25 Emergent Reader
Mini-Books

▲▲▲

Easy-to-Make Reproducible Books to Promote Literacy

by Maria Fleming

SCHOLASTIC
PROFESSIONAL BOOKS

NEW YORK • TORONTO • LONDON • AUCKLAND • SYDNEY

Interior design by Kathy Massaro
Cover design by Jaime Lucero and Vincent Ceci
Cover and interior illustrations by Abby Carter

ISBN: 0-590-33071-3

Contents

How to Use This Book

Here are reproducible patterns to make 25 mini-books that we hope will delight and engage your emerging readers as they strengthen their skills. The easy-to-make, easy-to-read books are designed to build children's confidence as readers and help them gain fluency.

The books are organized around popular elementary themes such as the seasons, the five senses, and all about me (see the Table of Contents for additional themes.) And while the stories increase in difficulty within the themed sections, they all include repetitive and often rhyming language, and follow predictable patterns. Each book's illustrations closely support the text to provide clues for emerging readers in decoding words.

How to Make the Mini-Books

1. Make a double-sided copy of the mini-book pages. Start by making a copy of the first page of the mini-book with the title page in the upper left-hand corner of the platen glass. Place this copy into the paper tray blank-side up. Again, check to be sure that the title page is in the upper left-hand corner. Then, place the second page on the platen glass with page 2 of the mini-book in the lower left-hand corner.

If your machine has a double-sided function and you would like to make copies this way, you'll need to remove the mini-book pages from the book.

Regardless of how you make the double-sided copies, you may need to experiment a bit to be sure that the pages are aligned properly, and that page 2 appears behind the title page.

2. Cut the page in half along the solid line and trim off the shaded portion of the page.

3. Place page 3 behind the title page.

4. Fold the pages in half along the dotted line.

5. Check to be sure that the pages are in the proper order and then staple them together along the book's spine.

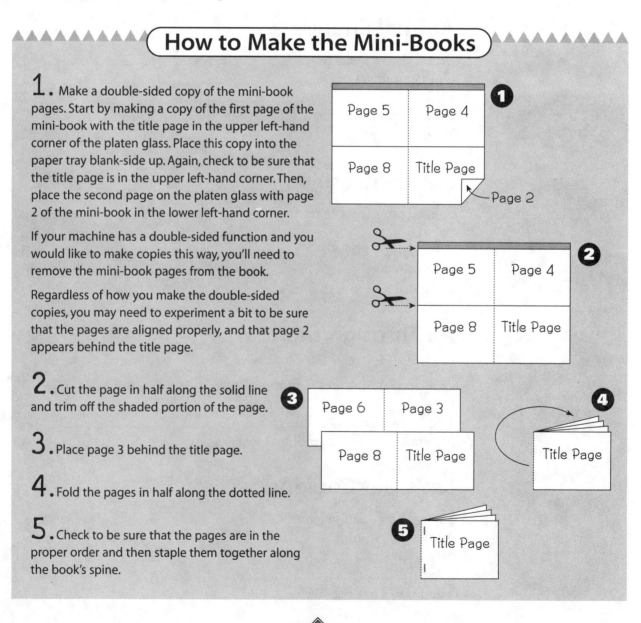

How to Use the Mini-Books

Supplement your current reading program with the reproducible books as needed—to reinforce a particular skill or to provide content reading on a theme your class is studying. The books can be used for shared reading, guided reading, paired or independent reading, and take-home reading. Following are suggestions for a sequence of activities intended to maximize the books' usefulness in skill-building.

Shared Reading: You may want to first use the books as part of a shared reading activity. Provide each child with a copy of one of the reproducible books. Working with the whole class, model a reading strategy as you move through the text of the book. For example, you may want to demonstrate how readers rely on picture clues or context cues to help decode text. Or, you may decide to isolate a phonics skill and offer a mini-lesson on it. For example, you might want to use a particular mini-book to:

♦ teach letter-sound relationships: i.e. the short *o* sound in the book "Lots of Spots" (p. 23), the short *u* sound in "Noisy Lunch" (p. 35), the initial *b* sound in "Bears, Bears, Bears" (p. 17), or the initial *p* sound in "The Pizza That Pete Made" (p. 55).

♦ teach initial clusters: i.e. the *s* blends in "I Can!" (p. 9) and "The Snowy Day" (p. 43); the *wh* digraph in "Who Is Sleeping?" (p. 25) and the *th* digraph in "The Pizza That Pete Made" (p. 55).

♦ teach inflections: i.e. the verb inflection *ing* in "Ears Hear" (p. 29) and "One Sun: A Summer Counting Book" (p. 39); the noun inflection *s* in "Best Friends"(p. 13) and "I'm Not Afraid of Anything!" (p. 15).

Because many of the stories rhyme, and thus contain similar spelling patterns, they are also helpful in teaching students to decode words by analogy. Many young children have trouble isolating each individual sound within a word, but they can divide words into *onset* (the initial consonant sound or sounds, i.e. *br* in bring) and *rime* (the vowel in a given syllable and what follows it, i.e. *ing* in bring). Students can use their prior knowledge of a spelling pattern in a familiar word to decode an unfamiliar word; for example, if they encounter the word sting for the first time in a book, they may be able to decode it by recognizing how it is similar to the known word bring. The rhyming text in the following mini-books would work particularly well with the analogy approach since the same spelling patterns are repeated in two or more words in the text: "I Can!" (p. 9), "Feelings" (p. 11), "Up in the Sky" (p. 33), "Ears Hear" (p. 29), "Super-Duper Sandwich" (p. 47), and "Apples All Around" (p. 49). (Note: It's a good idea to create a display of words with familiar spelling patterns on a wall or a bulletin board so that students can refer to them for help in decoding by analogy.)

Guided Reading: Following shared reading, you may want to divide students into small, homogeneous ability groups and give them an opportunity to apply the reading strategies you have modeled. Students can reread the same mini-book you used in the shared reading activity, or begin a new story.

Either way, engage them in a dialogue about the book before you begin to frame the reading experience that will follow. You may want to activate prior knowledge about the subject of the book, ask children to predict what might happen in the story, and/or point out any unusual elements in the text such as rhyming language or a repeated refrain. These discussions will help prepare children for the reading experience by introducing them to some of the words and ideas they may encounter in the book.

Following your introduction, allow children to move through the text on their own. Intervene with each child as necessary to provide support as they problem-solve their way through trouble spots in the text. Encourage children to employ more than one strategy to check for meaning and allow them to self-correct mistakes. Provide positive reinforcement when they use a strategy successfully. Use the guided reading sessions to assess an individual student's grasp of various strategies.

Independent Reading: After repeated exposures to a mini-book, it is likely that children will have mastered or nearly mastered the text. Reading specialists believe that books children read with 95 percent accuracy are ideal for independent reading. Such books provide students with an opportunity to build fluency and gain confidence as readers. Encourage independent reading by providing extra copies of the books in reading corners and theme-based learning centers. Children may want to read the books silently to themselves, share them with a partner, or respond to them in a reading journal. You also may want to have each child bring a

shoe box from home, which he or she can decorate and use to store the mini-books. Students will enjoy building their own personal library of books that they can read all by themselves. Having their own mini-book libraries will enable children to return to the books time and again for pure enjoyment and to remind them of their reading successes.

Take-Home Reading: Give children an opportunity to "show off" their reading successes for their families. Once children have mastered a story, give them a paper "Ask Me to Read...." medallion like the one shown below. Before children leave school for the day, pin the medallion to their shirt or jacket. The medallions will help promote pride in children for their developing proficiency as readers. They may also spur an invitation from someone at home to read the mini-book, further strengthening children's skills and confidence.

However you decide to use these books, we hope they help instill in your students a love of language and reading to last a lifetime.

4

people with short hair

5

people with curly hair

My Family

8

people who love each other

people with long hair

Who's in my family?

people with gray hair

people with no hair

I can run.

I can ride.

I Can!

I can do ANYTHING!

I can skip.

I can slide.

I can swing.

I can skate.

Some days I feel silly.

Feelings

Some days I feel mad.

Today I read a book by myself, and I feel proud!

Some days I feel sad.

Some days I feel happy.

Some days I feel loud.

Some days I feel quiet.

Best Friends

Best friends share cupcakes.

4

Best friends share secrets.

5

best friends share hugs!

8

Best friends share hats.

Best friends share books.

Best friends share presents.

But best of all,

I'm Not Afraid of Anything!

---

4 I'm not afraid of shots.

---

5 I'm not afraid of roller coasters.

---

8 Well, maybe a little.

I'm not afraid of snakes.

I'm not afraid of spiders.

I'm not afraid of thunder.

I'm not afraid of the dark.

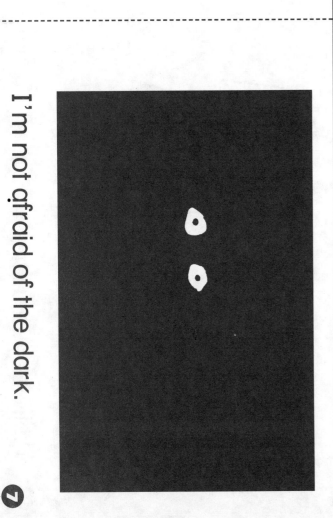

4

There are bears in snow.

Bears, Bears, Bears

5

There are bears in zoos.

8

Goodnight, bears.

There are bears in caves.

There are bears in trees.

There are bears in bed.

There are bears in books.

Penguins go in.

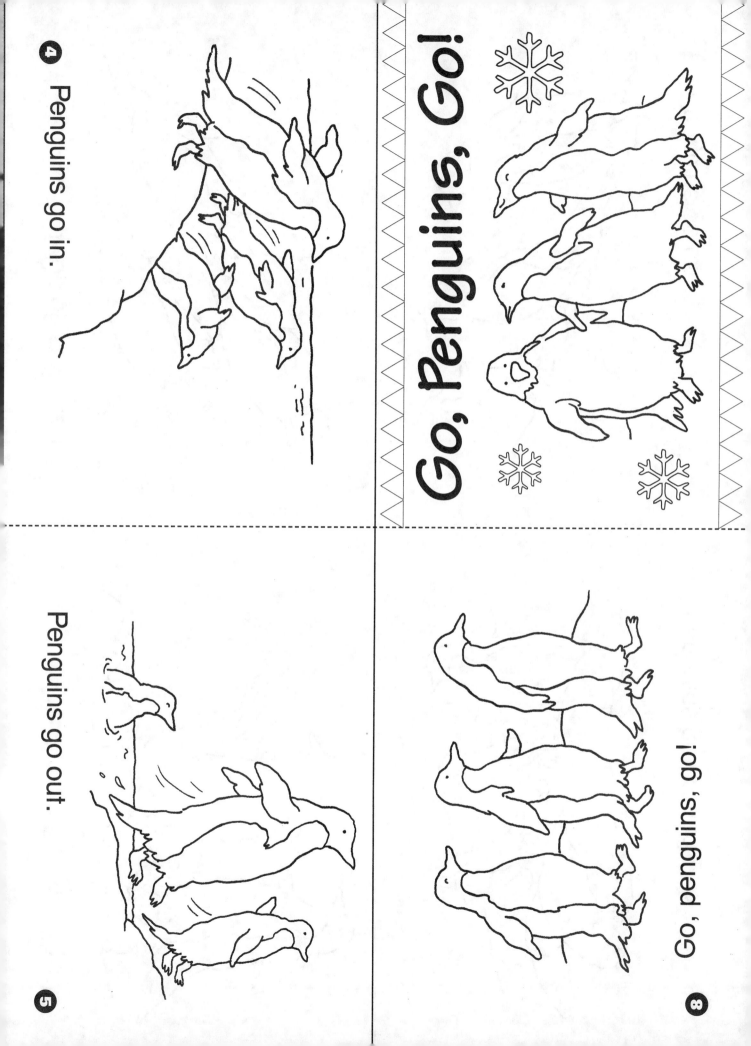

Go, Penguins, Go!

Penguins go out.

Go, penguins, go!

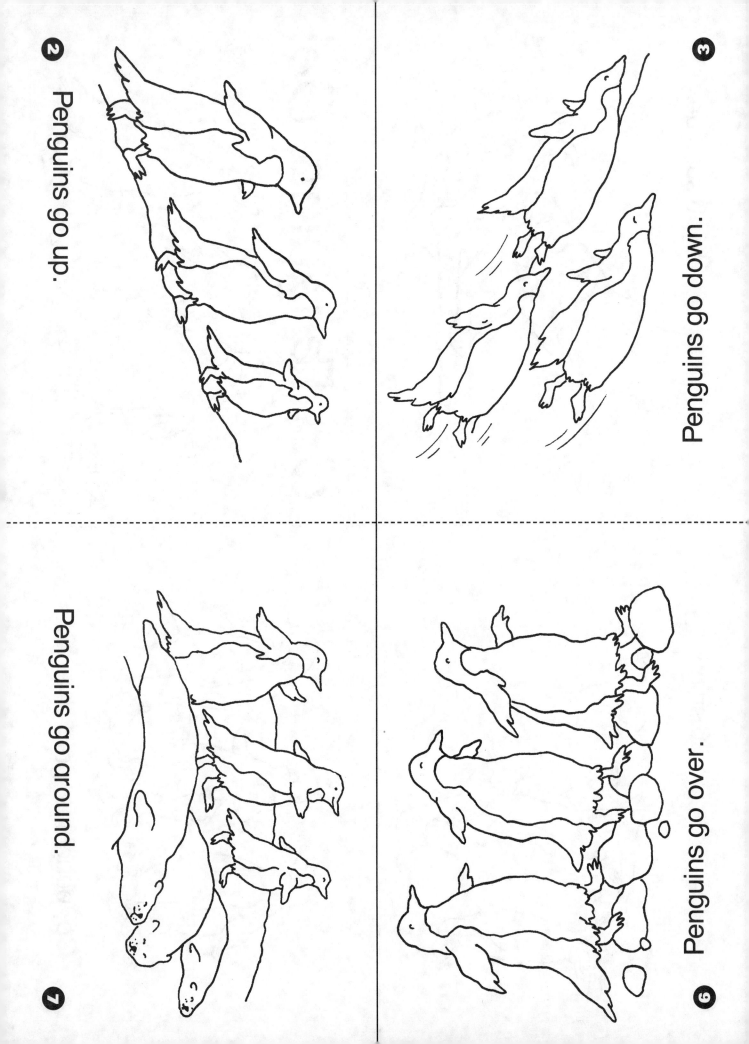

2

Penguins go up.

3

Penguins go down.

Penguins go around.

7

Penguins go over.

6

4

I like wet dogs.

I Like Dogs

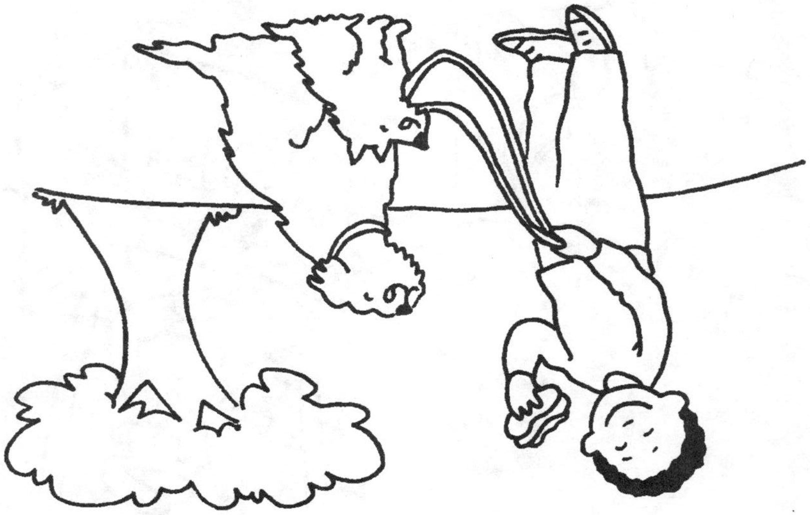

5

I like dry dogs.

hot dogs!

8

2

I like big dogs.

3

I like little dogs.

7

But I really like,

Hot Dogs

6

I like cold dogs.

A ladybug has spots.
Lots and lots.

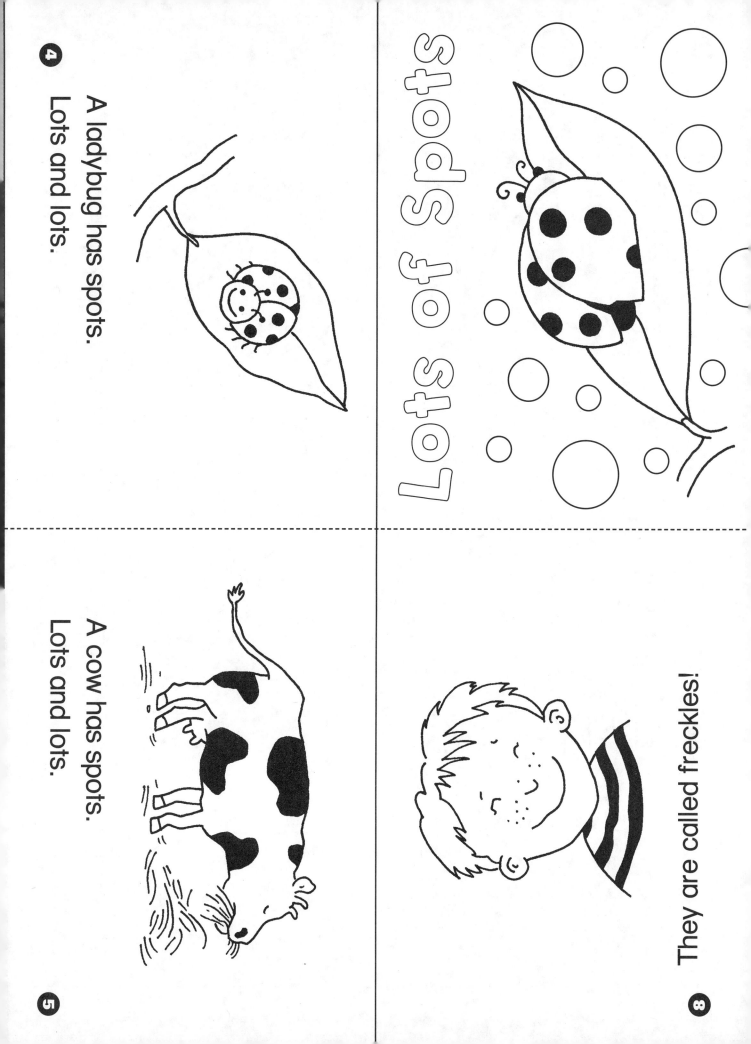

Lots of Spots

A cow has spots.
Lots and lots.

They are called freckles!

A leopard has spots.
Lots and lots.

A giraffe has spots.
Lots and lots.

My dog has spots.
Lots and lots.

I have spots, too.
Lots and lots.

Who Is Sleeping?

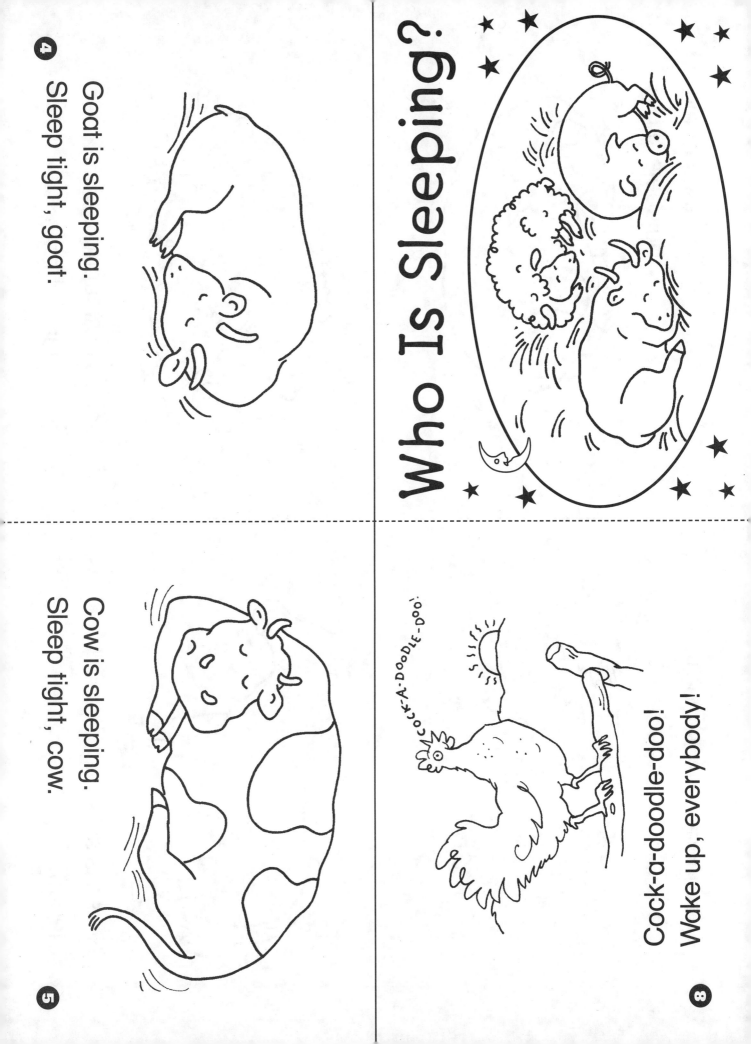

4

Goat is sleeping.
Sleep tight, goat.

5

Cow is sleeping.
Sleep tight, cow.

8

Cock-a-doodle-doo!
Wake up, everybody!

COCK-A-DOODLE-DOO!

Sheep is sleeping.
Sleep tight, sheep.

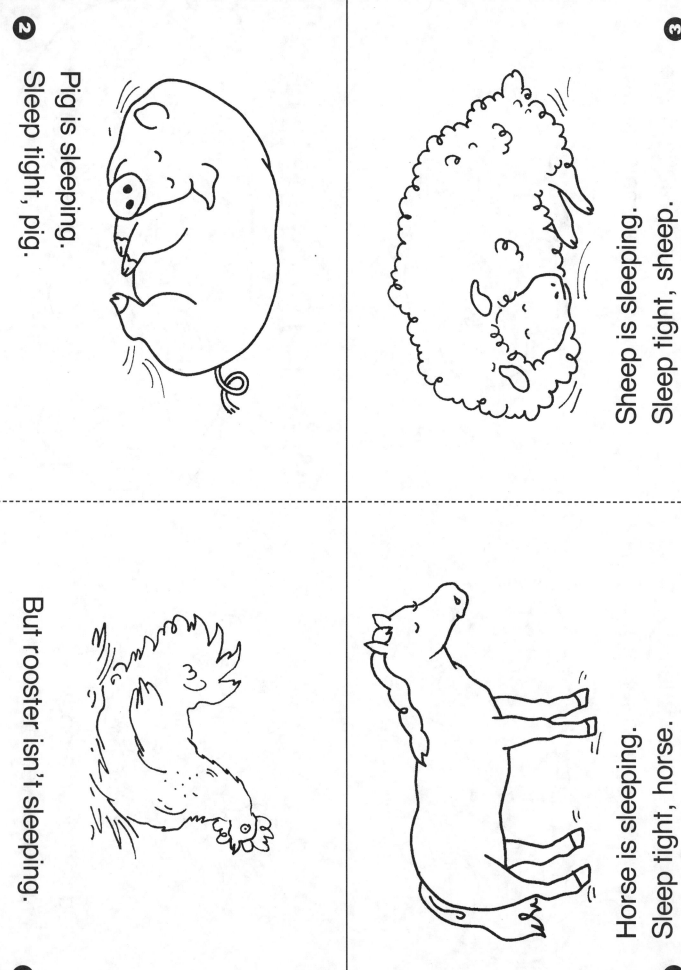

Pig is sleeping.
Sleep tight, pig.

Horse is sleeping.
Sleep tight, horse.

But rooster isn't sleeping.

4

My blanket feels soft. So soft.

Some Things
Feel Soft

My teddy bear feels soft. So soft.

5

My kitten feels soft.
So very, very soft.

8

My pajamas feel soft. So soft.

My pillow feels soft. So soft.

What else feels soft?

My sheets feel soft. So soft.

Ears hear planes zooming.

Ears Hear

Ears hear thunder booming.

KABOOM!

There's just no topping...... ears!

Ears hear people singing.

Ears hear phones ringing.

Ears hear dishes dropping.

Ears hear balloons popping.

Pizza smells good.

Flowers smell good.

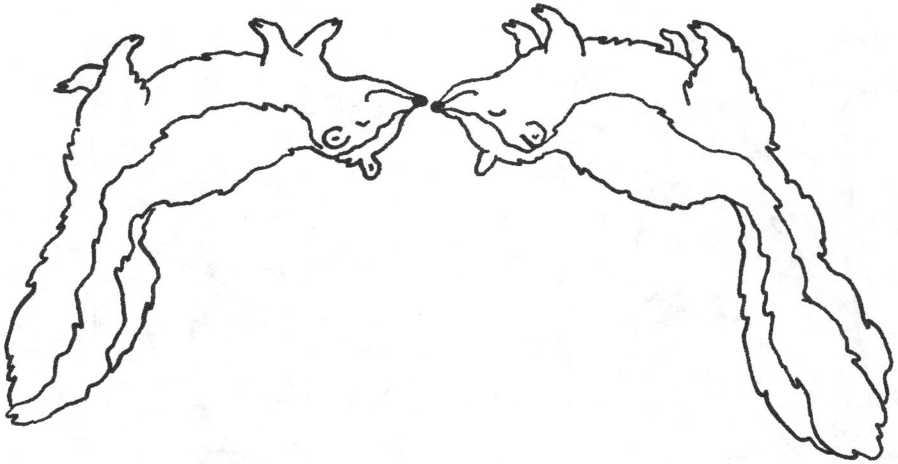

What Smells Good?

....to another skunk!

Soap smells good.

Pine trees smell good.

Cookies smell good.

A skunk smells good......

4

I see a cloud all fluffy white.

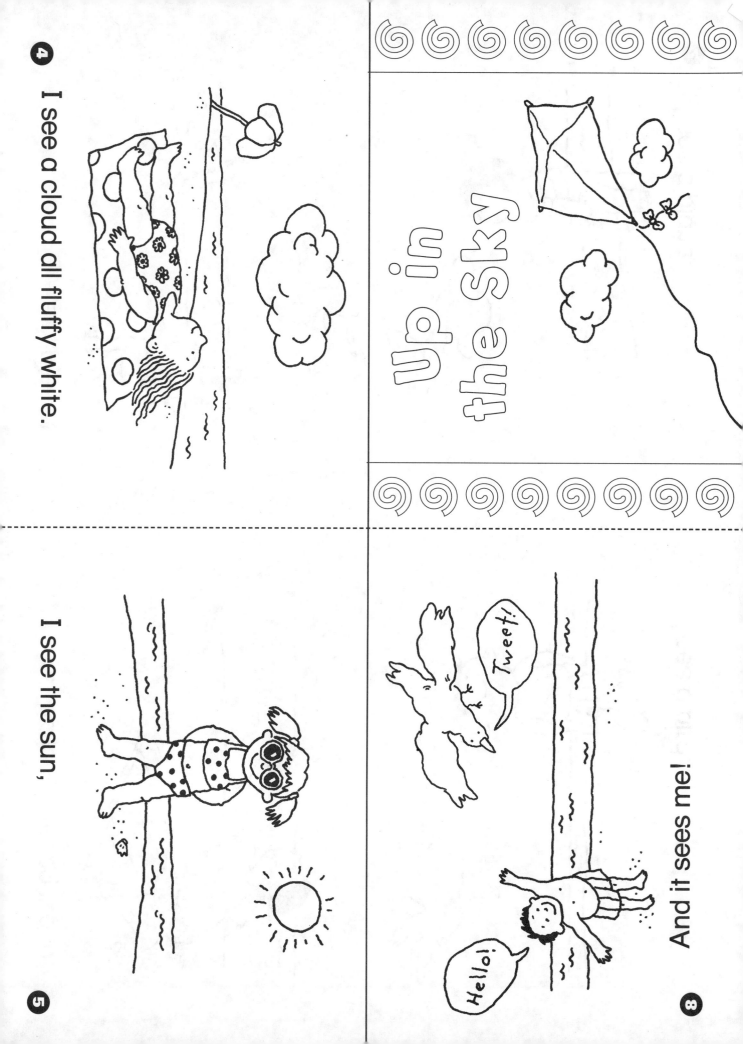

5

I see the sun,

Up in the Sky

And it sees me!

Tweet!

Hello!

8

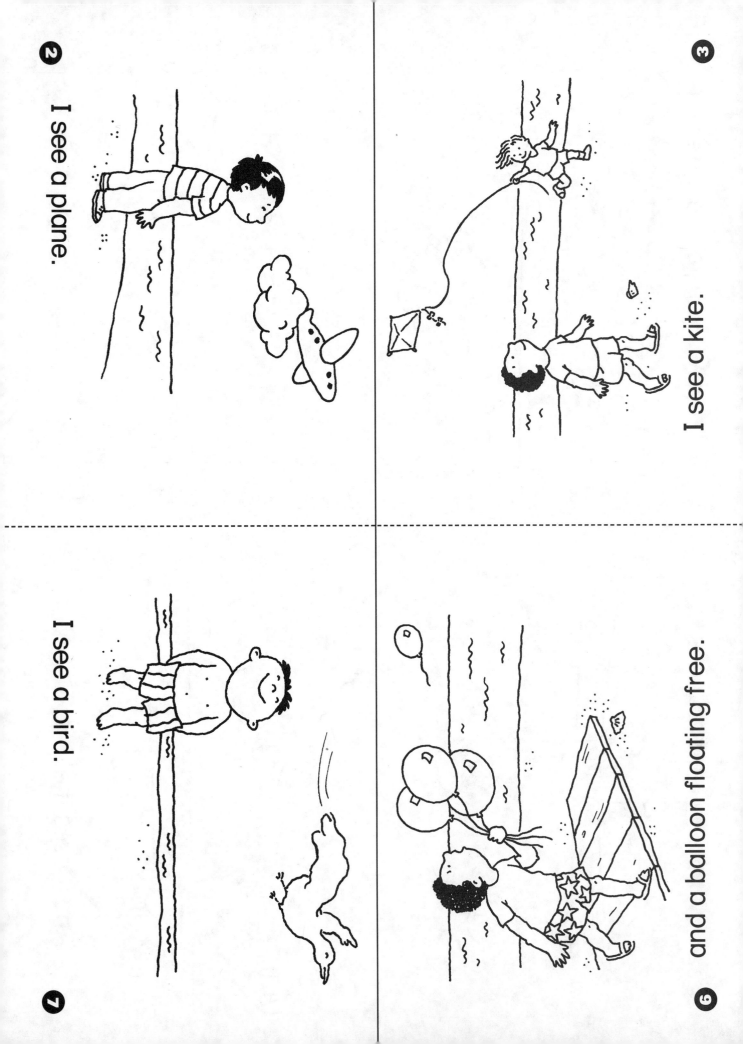

3

I see a kite.

2

I see a plane.

6 and a balloon floating free.

7

I see a bird.

Noisy Lunch

Munch, crunch. Munch, crunch.
Popcorn makes a noisy lunch.

4

Munch, crunch. Munch, crunch.
Celery makes a noisy lunch.

5

Munch, crunch. Munch, crunch.
Tomorrow bring a quiet lunch!

8

3

Munch, crunch. Munch, crunch.
Carrots make a noisy lunch.

2

Munch, crunch. Munch, crunch.
What things make a noisy lunch?

6

Munch, crunch. Munch, crunch.
Apples make a noisy lunch.

7

Munch, crunch. Munch, crunch.
Tacos make a noisy lunch.

4 new pencils

5 new teacher

Time for School

8 new friends

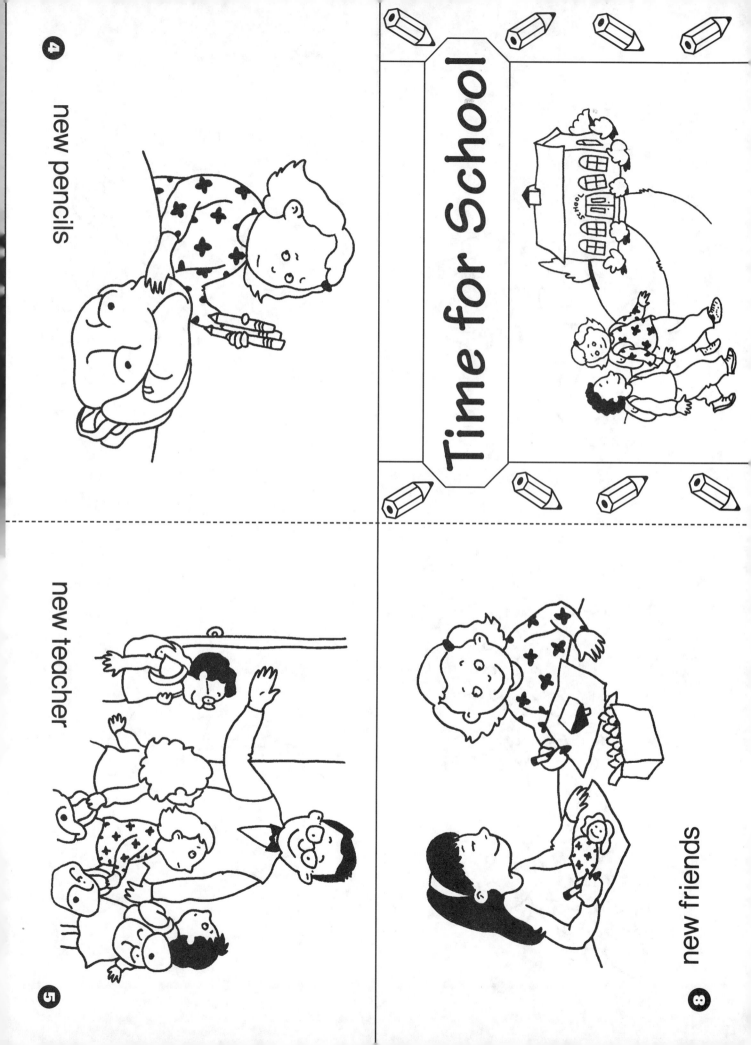

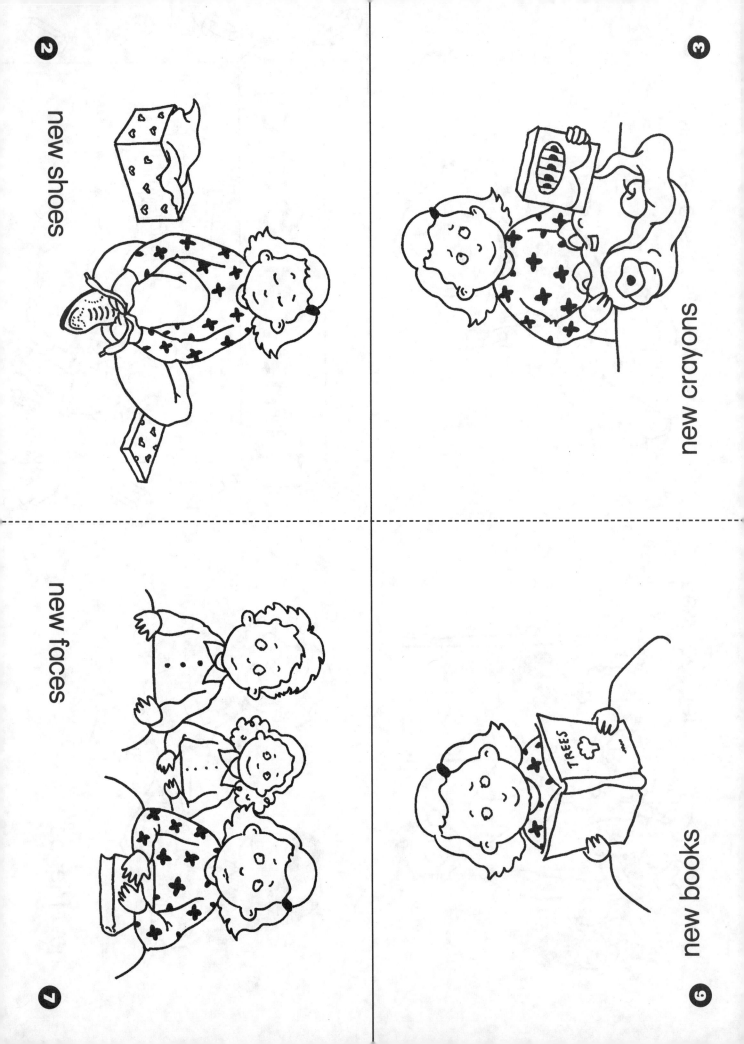

new shoes

new crayons

new faces

new books

4 Five dogs running.

One Sun:
A Summer Counting Book

Four boys splashing.

5

One sun shining.

8

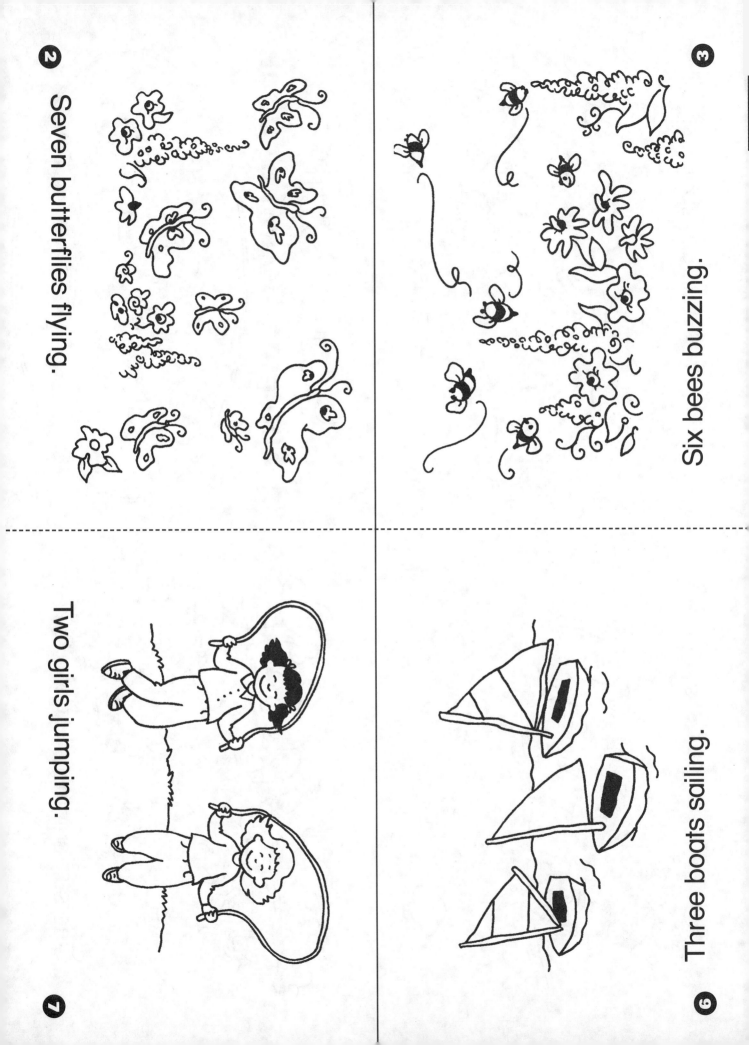

Seven butterflies flying.

2

Six bees buzzing.

3

Two girls jumping.

7

Three boats sailing.

6

Six birds in a tree.

Eight birds in a tree.

Birds in a Tree

Flying away from me!

Wooosh!

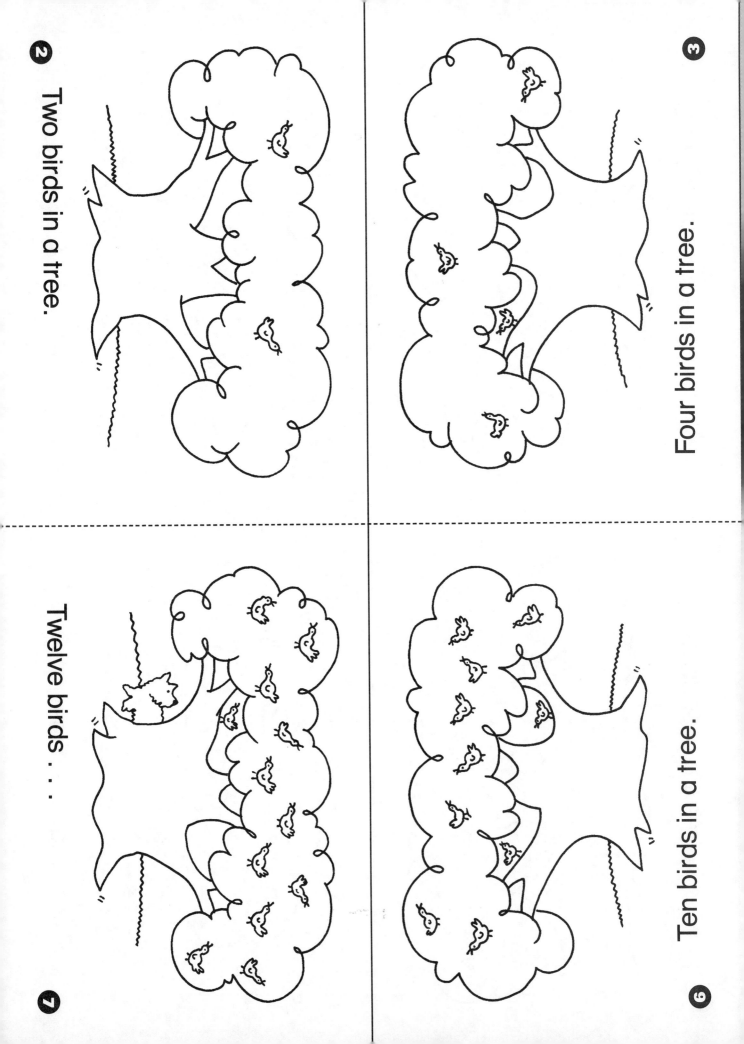

Four birds in a tree.

Two birds in a tree.

Ten birds in a tree.

Twelve birds . . . .

Where is my scarf?

The Snowy Day

Where are my boots?

Where is the snow?

Where is my hat?

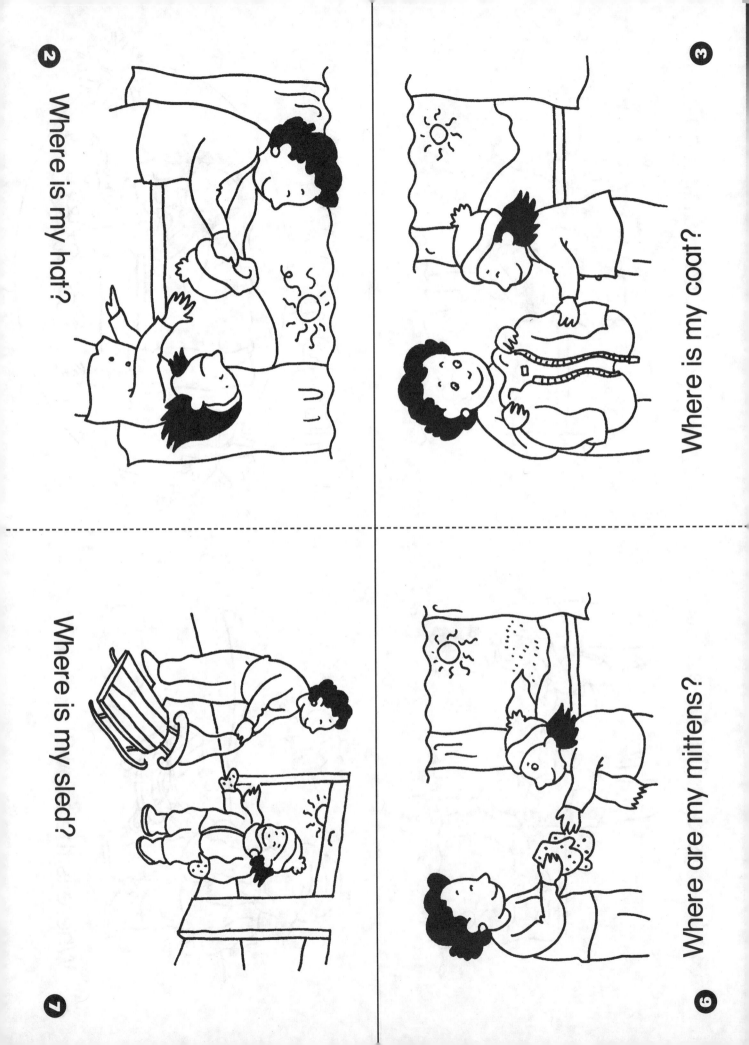

Where is my coat?

Where is my sled?

Where are my mittens?

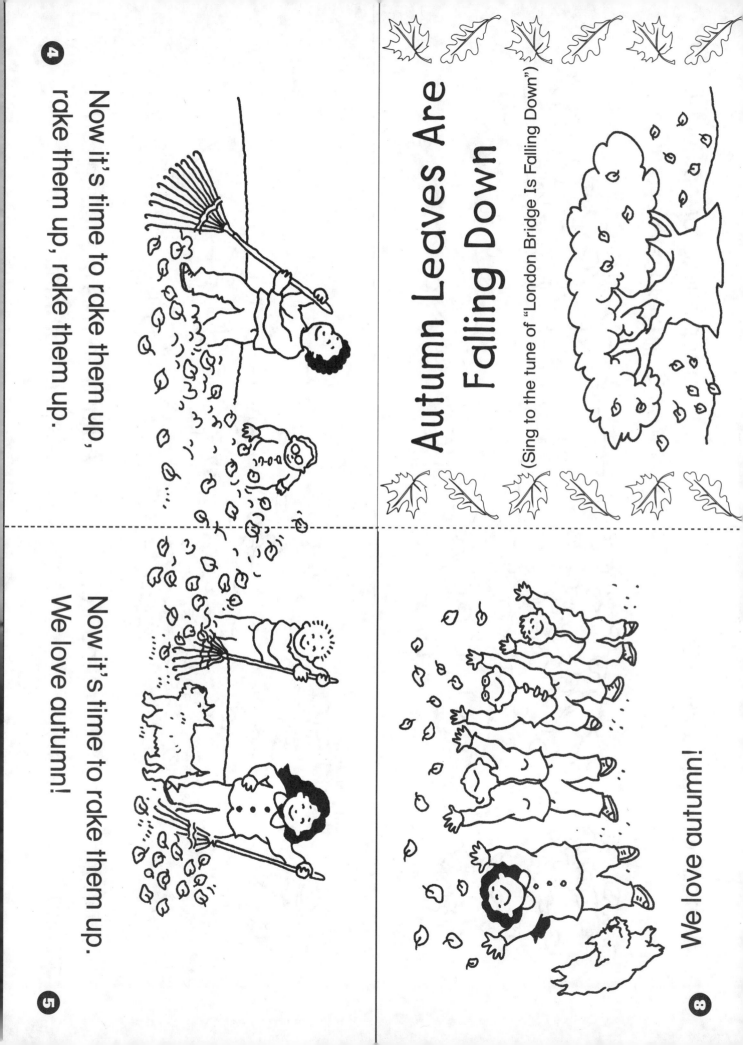

4

Now it's time to rake them up.
rake them up, rake them up.

5

Now it's time to rake them up.
We love autumn!

Autumn Leaves Are Falling Down

(Sing to the tune of "London Bridge Is Falling Down")

We love autumn!

8

Autumn leaves are falling down.
We love autumn!

Autumn leaves are falling down,
falling down, falling down.

Jump in them and roll around, roll around, roll around.

Jump in them and roll around.

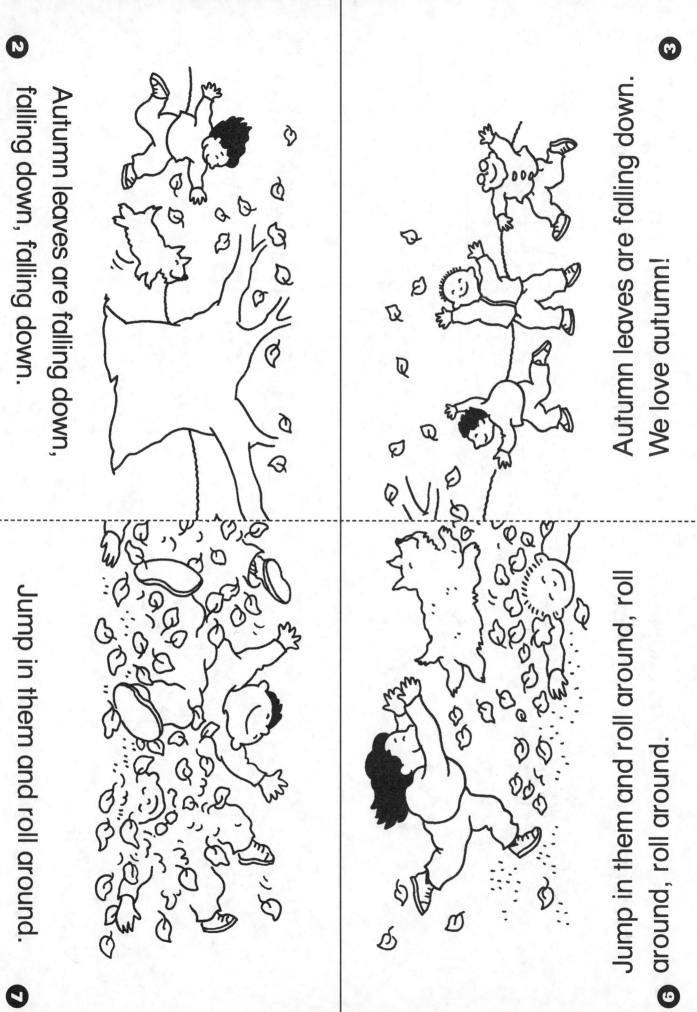

Then come the pickles.

Super-Duper Sandwich

Then comes the ham.

Then comes the stomachache.
No more for me, please!

Then comes the jam.

First comes the peanut butter.

Then comes the cheese.

Then come the jelly beans.

4

Apples on the ground.

Apples All Around

5

Apples in the store.

8

Apples in me.
Yum!

Apples in the air.

Apples, apples everywhere,
shiny, red, and round.

Apples in a tree.

Apples in an apple pie.

4

Add the eggs.
Add the milk.

Mix It Up!

5

Mix it up.
Mix it up.

8

Pour the batter.
Bake the muffins.
Eat them up.
Eat them up.

Mix it up.
Mix it up.

Pour the flour.
Pour the sugar.

Add the butter.
Add the berries.

Mix it up.
Mix it up.

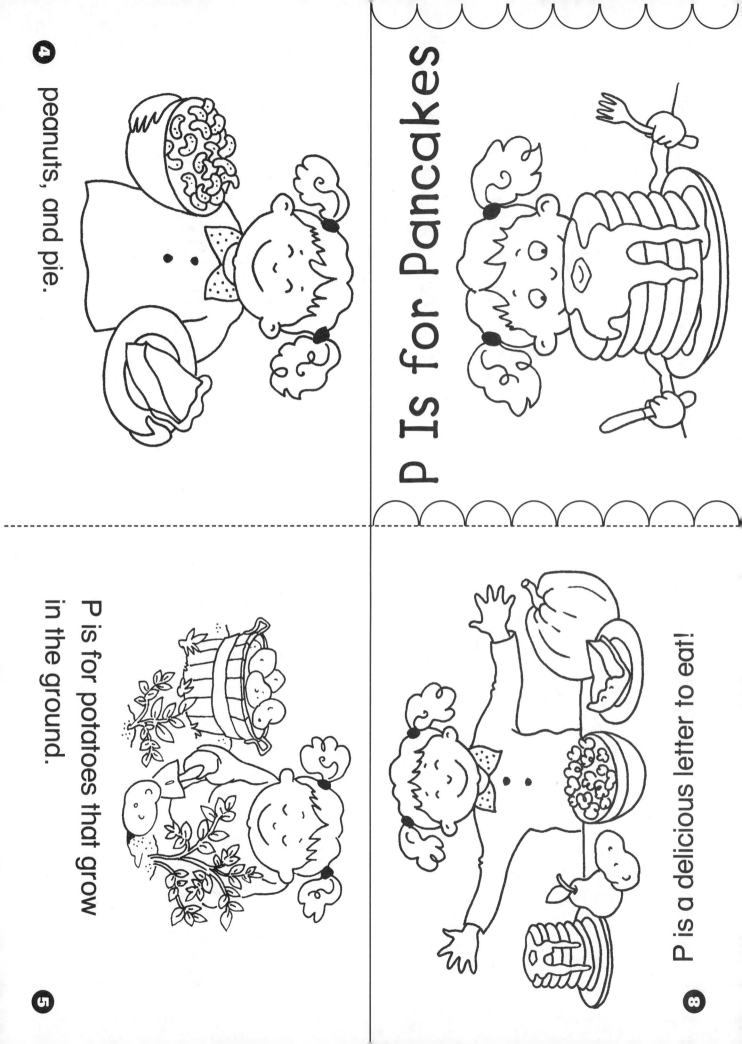

4

peanuts, and pie.

P Is for Pancakes

P is for potatoes that grow
in the ground.

5

P is a delicious letter to eat!

8

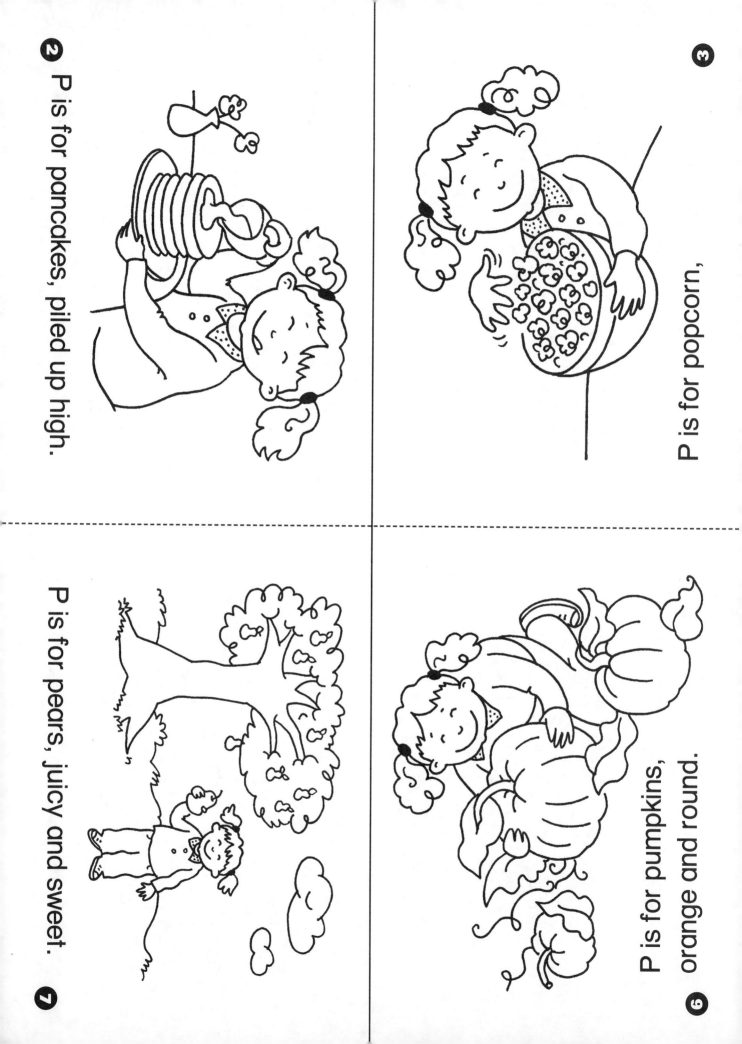

2 P is for pancakes, piled up high.

3 P is for popcorn,

7 P is for pears, juicy and sweet.

6 P is for pumpkins, orange and round.

4

This is the cheese that went on the pizza that Pete made.

The Pizza That Pete Made

5

These are the mushrooms that went on the pizza that Pete made.

8

Thanks, Pete!

3

This is the sauce that went on the pizza that Pete made.

2

This is the pizza that Pete made.

6

This is the oven that cooked the pizza that Pete made.

7

These are the friends that ate the pizza that Pete made.